Earth
Journey

A Guide to Living with the Seasons

KRISTA THORNHILL
EDITED BY KALYN SLOAN

◆ FriesenPress

Suite 300 - 990 Fort St
Victoria, BC, V8V 3K2
Canada

www.friesenpress.com

First Printing: 2017

Earth Based Spirit Ministries
Salt Spring Is. BC V8K 1P6

www.kristathornhill.com

ISBN
978-1-5255-6093-4 (Hardcover)
978-1-5255-6094-1 (Paperback)
978-1-5255-6095-8 (eBook)

1. BODY, MIND & SPIRIT, GAIA & EARTH ENERGIES

Distributed to the trade by The Ingram Book Company

Praise for Earth Journey

"Tracing a transpersonal path through the seasons, *Earth Journey* guides the reader through the year with suggestions for connecting with the many faces of Gaia through cross cultural celebrations, personal reflection and ritual. This engaging primer is a threshold into earth spirituality for all who want to walk a path attuned with nature and the sacred feminine. Both poetic and practical, you'll feel you are sitting at Thornhill's kitchen table with a cup of herbal tea with this comforting and inspiring guide".

Danielle Blackwood, author of The Twelve Faces of the Goddess: Transform Your Life with Astrology, Magick and the Sacred Feminine

Earth Journey was my introduction to Gaia and by the time I finished the book I felt as if I had been friends with her all along. This is a beautifully written book, written by a talented author who is able to write about practical spirituality in a way that made me feel like I was having tea with a friend. This book was a pleasure to read.

~Stephanie Anne Clair, Fox Creek Alberta

Krista's guide Earth Journey, invites us into the physical realm of spirituality, one governed by seasons and elemental forces: where the profound and spirit are all around us, earth bound. A refreshingly practical approach to anchor one's self, as this is also an invitation to explore the depths within. A book crafted to suite any stage of life: to journey alone or with your family. Earth Journey offers a hands on method to restore one's rhythm to the very pulse of our Mother Planet.

~Luna Sharpe, Salt Spring Is. BC

In Earth Journey, Krista Thornhill invites us to remember we are not strangers in the house of Gaia, the Earth. Wrapping us in a shawl of poetic language, she inspires us with stories of her family's seasonal traditions and guides us to create our own.

Like the Earth Hostess herself, Krista's hospitality is wise, deep and nourishing. Through each month's multi-dimensional teachings, she offers us a playful, spirit full guide to realigning with the creative flow of the year.

Krista teaches us how to keep our eyes and ears, nose, mouths and hands open to the elemental gifts of Gaia and to find our own ground within Her ever changing seasons.

As I turned the pages, I felt reassured in my belonging to this wild, beautiful planet while curious to read on and discover what further elemental wisdom she would bring me.

Earth Journey is a sumptuous guide for awakening self-love and authentic Earth Connection.

~Ahava Shira, PhD, Poet, Beloved Earth Daughter and author of Womb: Weaving of My Being, Love is Like This and Co-author of Writing Alone Together: Journaling in a Circle of Women for Creativity, Compassion and Connection.

Dedication

To my loving knight in shining armor, Gerald Stel who has been unwavering in his support and enthusiasm for all my projects. I am so blessed to share my journey with you. You are the bravest man I know!

TABLE OF CONTENTS

Acknowledgements

I would like to acknowledge the powerful influence that my beautiful grandmother, Colleen Poole May, had upon my life. She taught me how to live royally, how to love honestly and how to have mountain moving faith. Our love for each other was unlike any other. She is not resting in peace, but dancing up a storm waiting for us all to join her.

Colleen, by Krista Thornhill, 1992

Foreword

When we align ourselves with the turning of the Earth, live every month with the seasons, and find our way on this journey acknowledging that we are humans having an Earth experience, we open up to a natural flow like no other. No longer shall we be amiss in the cosmos of reality, discombobulated and feeling foreign in a strange land or in a disconnected state of being, but rather we shall be grounded, solid in our steps, fully conscious, and awake in every moment.

If we re-learn the ways of old, recycle old tools, and repurpose old philosophies, then add a modern twist that is personal and real, we can re-discover what is innately common, the one thing that unites us all: we are spirits having an Earth experience in human form.

There is no better guide for this journey than our Earthly Hostess, whose lessons and guidance have been here all along, showing us the way. The Seasons have guided us and influenced our lives whether we have been conscious of it or not; we have been living every day in relationship with the greatest Hostess one could ever imagine.

In this book, we will look at what it means to journey on this planet having an Earth experience. We will go month to month, checking in with the Earth as she moves through the light and dark halves of the year. We will look at ways in which we can fall in sync with her, internally and externally. As we go we will be implementing great love and compassion for ourselves and for this beautiful and wonderful Hostess of ours.

This is not a self-help book, but rather a personal guide for living in season.

If we can agree, to start, that the Earth is feminine (in that she is a producer, feeder, nourisher, and giver), then we can build on that concept with the personification of a female character, thus making the Earth relatable and tangible. A character that, like us, develops and changes over time from child to maiden, mother to queen, and queen to crone. In each of these phases of her life, she experiences the seasons and the elements as we do.

She is playful like the child when the Wind catches hold of a falling feather and playfully wisps it about. She is perky as the maiden coming into her sexuality when tulips and daffodils break forth from the soil. She is the mother when she sacrifices herself for her children and lets them take more than they should. She is the queen who rages over the waters, who floods the land and drowns the cattle. She is the old crone, the patient and wise grandmother who bends down her tired branches so that we may climb into her arms, draw closer to her heartbeat and listen to her stories. It is she who will, in the end, lay down her life so that new life can be born to her lineage, so that the story may continue as she embraces death and dies, again and again.

The key element to grasp when starting on this path is that her time is not our time. It is neither linear nor circular, but spiral, ever expanding outwards as the wheel turns. Think of the Fibonacci spiral, for as the Earth turns, she is moving ever outwards as she spins following the sun's movement through the galaxy, unfixed in one set position.

We cannot fit her schedule into ours, for although our traditional holidays do for the most part fall in line with the seasons, she operates within her own structures. In this book we will learn that our human-made constructs of time only sometimes line up with the Earth's rotations; we don't always get spring showers in May and we don't always get snow for Christmas. The more we can align with her, the better we can adapt to the inconsistencies of our lives. Here we will explore her individual timings, manifested through the seasons and affected by the elements.

She has strong characteristics that can be defined as the four elements: Earth, Air, Fire, and Water. She is courageous, fearless and passionate, as the element of Fire. She is powerful, loving, nurturing and just, as the element of Water. She is grounded, peaceful, practical, firm, and hardworking, as the element of Earth. She is playful, wise, ancient and discerning, as the element of Air.

Introducing Gaia

God was a Woman, Bev Yeoman's Chair, by Krista Thornhill, 2013

Introducing Gaia

Allow me to tell you about this wonderful dear old friend of mine, Gaia. Even though she may appear to be quite old, don't be fooled, this woman grows younger every day. She is spry and active, constantly doing new things to keep ahead of the times. She is creative and unpredictable, continuously doing renovations to her house, like adding rooms, changing wallpapers, and moving furniture. Even her houseguests seem to change frequently. She loves this life; it keeps her young she says. The activity seems to ignite something within her and to get to know her has truly ignited something inside of me. When you go into her house, you might as well take off your watch, for she operates on her own time, and if you get pancakes for dinner at three in the afternoon, well that's just like getting a dumping of snow in June.

Gaia amazes me: she is tenacious and versatile, always ready to change and adapt to whatever is happening. I wish to be just as flexible! Gaia has had many children, and although they have all grown up and moved on, they will often return to visit, bringing grandchildren, great-grandchildren and so forth. She will proudly reveal the scars of stretch marks to anyone who seeks proof that she has birthed so many, and, laughingly, she will remark about her sagging breast having nourished multitudes. I love her sense of humour, though I can't help but feel a little sad to see the effects of childbearing on her body, as part of me grieves that younger body of mine. None-the-less, when you are with

Gaia, it is hard to feel sorry for yourself; she's got no time for that bullshit. She is busy getting on with getting on, for the bread is in the oven, the garden overflows with the fruits of her magical green thumb, and she's talking permaculture with her roommates Gravid (gravity) and Electra (electricity).

Getting to know Gaia, I have noticed and grown to expect the seasonal changes to her personality. In the fall, a quietness comes over her as she tends to talk a lot about the past. She tells tales of the many children that have come and gone with a sweet sense of nostalgia. She darkens the house with thick curtains, stocks the woodpile closer to the house and begins to store her food for the winter. I have often caught her out in the yard playing with the Wind, one of her closest friends. They are hilarious together, and you can tell when they get out of hand because tree branches start to fall to the ground and church bells start ringing.

In the fall, Gaia will serve you hot apple cider and pumpkin pie when you come to visit. You are bound to hear a ghost story or two. She loves company and a good game of chess. She'll wrap a shawl around your shoulders and will ask you who your ancestors are and where you come from. She will nod as you tell her your story, as she remembers it all as you tell her, for you are not a stranger in her house, you are as one of her own, and you cannot help but feel safe and loved.

The darker the season grows, the more withdrawn Gaia becomes. She says, "Just like cold molasses, I don't move too quickly without the heat." If ever there is a time when I feel her age, it is at this time of year; I cannot help but worry for her and I want to connect with her all the more. I have learned you can join her by the Fire, but expect little conversation, for though she is a good listener, her mind is far away, focused on deep internal things, like letting go of all that she has created. She is grieving for her youth, for her children that have come and gone, for the sadness they experienced on their journey and for all the times they did not come to visit her. Deep in these winter months, darkness seems to overcome her, and I feel the distance of my dear friend as she goes through what she must. I know now, I have nothing to worry about: this is just what she goes through in the dark half of the year.

Spring seems to be the best medicine for Gaia! She throws the curtains back and lets in all the morning light as it arrives earlier every morning. She washes everything with Water from her well. You can't help but be inspired as impulsiveness comes over her: things are sprouting and popping up all over the place, and she gets busier than a bee as the heat warms her up. "Like hot molasses running downhill!" She laughs as she sweeps winter debris away from her front door. She reminds me of *Alice in Wonderland*'s White Rabbit at the tea party, bustling about with much to do.[1] Mind you she is never late, for she has all the clocks in her house set to her own timing. Best not forget that, especially when coming to visit, for you will always arrive at just the right moment and she will always be delighted to see you, even if she can't stop what she's doing when you arrive. Also, don't expect to sit long and digest great conversation with her at this time! No, rather you should expect to be following her around the house and into the garden, talking as you go, lifting and carrying when needed. Her step is lighter as she dances across the kitchen floor singing a tune or whistling a ditty. With each turn closer to summer she grows more childlike, more playful, staying up later at night in the garden, talking until wee hours in the morning, staying up all night with the moon. And every spring she falls in love

---

1 Lewis Carroll, "Alice in Wonderland," in *Lewis Carroll: The Complete Works* (London: CRW Publishing Limited, 2005), 13-47.

again, guaranteed, for it doesn't matter how old she is, some young man will come into her life, and she will start to blush like a young maiden. It is quite sweet to watch. The way she swoons over new love makes you believe that you can stay young forever. She changes her style to soft vintage dresses for tea parties in the late afternoon, where she paints oils on canvas in the sunroom and drinks martinis in silk dressing gowns. She smokes her own herbs from a long glass pipe and will serve you a dose of psilocybin tea if she thinks you need it. She really is my kind of lady.

Gaia changes again come summer. In June she's not quite as much fun as she was in early spring, for she becomes very focused on the work that needs doing. She is set to tending the crops, weeding, watering, preparing, restoring, and staying up late working in the evening sun. She changes out of her lacy dresses and dons her overalls and baseball cap. She drives the tractor even still at her age. She runs the cattle and shears the sheep. Gaia is a hardworking woman with dirt on her face, broken fingernails and grass stains on her knees. "Got to walk the walk, do the work!" She calls out to me from the lawnmower. I love being around her at this time: she makes me feel like I can get things done, that I have the power! She says it's the sun's intense gift of energy that keeps her going, and I don't doubt her for a second, for she moves about with the confidence and assurance of a young mother set in motion! Stand out of her way: she's getting stuff done! Towards the end of the summer, you can see the change come over her as she finally tires herself out and starts to slow down. "They don't call it the dog days of summer for nothing," she laughs as she puts her feet up, wipes the soil from her face and takes a slow drink with me on the patio in the setting sun. She has earned this rest, and she takes it, teaching me to celebrate after the work is done, that to everything there is a season.

Come summer's end she becomes ever mindful of the harvest. Gathering each crop as they ripen, she plucks, trims, hangs, shucks, bottles, jams and picks all while planning a great celebration feast where everyone is welcome to join. She starts making plans for the year's end, completing tasks and getting the last of the outdoor chores done. She sees to the filling of the woodshed, the pantry, and the larder. She is mindful, quieter and often caught up in thought. Appearing to be hard of hearing, you can tell that she is beginning to feel older as she seems to be somewhat slipping away.

Then October comes, and suddenly you feel that she has grown old, older than you had realized, for she now draws heavy shawls over her shoulders and mutters under her breath about her aching bones in the damp air. She keeps the wood stove going, baking bread in the oven and always a pot of water ready for boiling. She is the hunter, the skinner, and the butcher and preps her winter pantry of dried fish and smoked meat. She is organized, particular, and very much on time. She is prepared and ready; it seems as if she is getting ready to die, for her house is in order.

I can't help but feel a little sadness to see my friend in such beautiful surrender. I'm sad because I remember the times when she was full of life, of how much fun she was in her youth, of all her mothering and bossiness, of her cooking and the way she takes care of everyone. She sees that I'm feeling these things and this is when I love my friend the most, for she puts her cool silken hand to my cheek and she says, "just you wait 'till I'm reborn!" and she gently laughs as she pats my face tenderly. "My death will be nothing compared to my rebirth. Now that," she declares, "will truly be something!"

The Earth Table: A Place for Gaia

An Earth Table, much like a home altar, is a special place in your home. Like a fireplace can be considered the heart of a home, the Earth Table would be the Earth centre of your home, a seasonally changing and sacred space to pay homage and respect to our great Hostess.

On it, place items of sacred importance to you and invite family members to do the same. A good place to start is with four things that are constant throughout the seasons that are the basic representations of the elements: a feather for Air, a vessel for Water, a candle for Fire and a rock for Earth. As you move through the chapters in this book, you will find a list of things that you can add to your Earth Table each month.

Whenever I am out for a walk, I always keep my eye open for little gifts from Gaia. One early spring morning, I found an eagle feather on the side of the road, sticking right up from the grass, just at the very moment I was congratulating myself for getting out for a walk in the morning rain. The feather was like receiving a gift from Gaia, an award for getting out of the house and coming to visit. It now adorns my Earth Table.

Seasonal Elements

To everything there is a season, and I like to think that there is also an element for every season. With each month, I have included the element that I connect with in hopes that you may find resonance with them as well. Please feel free to make your own associations, as many different practices do.

As the season changes in October, the winds of change begin to blow, and it becomes time to let go and allow death to do its thing. I slow down too and breathe more deeply as I prepare to settle into the dark months. I associate Air with the East, and the East with the past, my ancestors, and the road on which I've travelled. I remember my loved ones that I have let go of, all the things they have taught me and impressed upon me and the wisdom I have gained from having had them in my life. In December, I celebrate them along with family traditions as we welcome hope and

The Green Family's Earth Table, by Krista Thornhill, 2015

... the rebirth of the sun. We can journey through the months of October, November, and December connecting with and honouring the element of Air.

The Fire months are January, February, and March. These long dark nights give me time to work on myself, to dig deep into personal issues and to expose the cracks. I need courage and passion to examine my life closely, and for that, I sit as often as I can by the fire, inside and outside. We can journey through these months connected with and honouring the element of Fire.

Spring brings the rain and causes the creek beside my house to run fast and hard. It is a time to cleanse, renew, and revive; to wash the ashes off my skin and the smell of smoke out of my hair; to soothe and nurse the burns from winter's Fire; to be baptized and reborn. We can journey through April, May and June connected with and honouring the element of Water.

There is no other season that makes us more tactile with Gaia than the summer. Warm days allow us to walk barefoot on the earth and put our hands in the dirt. We swim in her warm waters, bask in the heat of the sun and live with comfort off of the land. Celebrating the element of Earth in July, August, and September, when we are the most active outside, gives us a practical experience of the element and reminds us to walk the walk, to live out daily what we believe, to apply everything that we have learned and to reach out to others.

***

I start our Earth Journey in the month of November, but you may jump to where ever you are in the calendar year and start your journey there. November symbolizes the day after death and thus is considered throughout pagan history as the Witch's New Year, for it marks our life like no other day... a very good place to start.

NOVEMBER: TO REMEMBER

Element of Air

Poppy and his wife Eudora walking through Ruckle Park, by Krista Thornhill, 2016

For the Earth Table: feathers and incense, poppies, photos of Ancestors

November: To Remember

To stop what we are doing and to remember, to recall, to retrace the steps taken before us, to remember the stories, names, cultures, languages and the religions of our makeup is the beginning of finding our own grounding in this Earth experience. It gives us a starting point, when we may not know where else to turn. If we start with healing the past, unpacking the baggage, and focusing on what needs to change, our journey becomes so much lighter, easier, and things begin to flow. We know where we are going; we journey on into healing and wholeness, living this life experience to its fullest, unencumbered by the past.

THE INTERNAL JOURNEY

Our Ancestral Story

If we don't know our ancestral roots, where we are coming from and with what skills and challenges we have inherited, we wander through life without a map. Our maps lead us towards healing and growth; they point us in the correct direction for optimum experience while laying out all the options. The best place to begin any journey is at the beginning.

I grew up with alcoholism, devote fundamental Christianity and promiscuity. Since I know my family story, I am able to look at my life to see the remnants of these influences on me and my Earth journey. I am always conscious of these things and am working to heal and redeem myself from influences of addiction, radicalism, and trust issues.

When I looked even further back into my Ancestral Story, I found Susan Poole, a white witch, known and respected in her community as a healer, a medicine woman. [2] She spoke to the dead, made herbal healing concoctions and read tea leaves. Finding her in my Ancestral Story has helped me find my power all the more, for I am just like her! Now I can truly say, "It runs in the family!"

Be careful not to throw the baby out with the bathwater when blazing new trails, for everything we learn and experience has value. Remember that our history serves a purpose and that we should think wisely about what we make redundant; we never know what we will face along the way and where some of those old tools may come in handy.

In Canada, November 11th is the National Day of Remembrance, where a full minute of silence is shared by everyone to honour the sacrifices of our foremothers and forefathers, and to honour the men and women who presently risk their lives to stand on the front lines for peace. We as a country remember. As communities, families, individuals, and leaders, we honour the past; we remember what war costs, and because we remember, we strive to live in peace all the more.

Memory Exercises

It's important to make time to remember; memory is a vital tool in our tool box. There is no such thing as a bad memory but rather lazy

---

2 Medicine Woman: a healer who uses native plants as medicine and harnesses the elements to aid the healing process.

ones. Since the brain believes whatever you tell it,[3] if you say, "I have a bad memory" or "I'm terrible at remembering people's names," the brain will manifest exactly that, leaving you with an excuse to let your memory skills slide. The brain, like the lungs and heart, is an organ designed to function at optimum levels: when we don't exercise our brain it gets lazy, and when it gets lazy, we get dull. It's important to keep our brains healthy and our minds sharp so that we can be alert to Gaia's ways of communication. Practice memory-building skills, begin to reprogram your mind and tell your brain to start remembering.

The next time you meet someone new, consider trying to take an extra-long moment to connect with them personally and say their name several times out loud. Allow your brain to mentally program their name with the visual of them and their energy into your memory files.

THE EXTERNAL JOURNEY

Air

In traditional craft practice, Air is the element of the East, associated with thought and mind, the rising sun, inspiration, and enlightenment.[4] Air is the breath of the Goddess,[5] Her living inspiration.[6] When you have a moment or two, stop what you're doing and face east. Best done on a very windy day, ask for the winds of inspiration and wisdom to blow down upon you. If there is something you are struggling with,

---

3 Rudolph E. Tanzi and Deepak Chopra, *The Super Brain* (New York: Three Rivers Press, 2012).

4 craft: how one chooses to incorporate their beliefs into their lifestyle and manifest their desires

5 Goddess: polytheistic worship of the divine feminine in human/deified form

6 Starhawk, *The Earth Path: Grounding Your Spirit in the Rhythms of Nature* (New York: Harper San Francisco, 2004), 77.

offer it up to the Air. Ask for guidance and revelation. Stand still and quiet in your meditation and feel the Air upon your skin, in your hair, moving through your clothes. Recognize the force of power at play. As you breathe in deeply to your lungs' full capacity, imagine you are taking into yourself the wisdom and teachings of your Ancestry. When you exhale, imagine that you are releasing all that has kept you bound and restricted. When finished, express gratitude to those that have gone before you and to the element of Air that sustains you.

Make time for deep breathing exercises and connect with the life-giving power of Air.

Witches New Year: November First

Witches traditionally celebrate this day as their New Year, marking the new beginning the day after All Hallows Eve. They believe that life comes after death and the cycle continues.

For those of us who have experienced the death of a loved one, we know that our lives begin on a very different path the day after, one without our loved one. It's a day that needs surrendering to; it's the day that marks the rest of our lives like no other can. Despite the darkest hole left in our hearts, life carries on, a new day begins, the wheel continues to turn, and the witches celebrate a new year!

On this day, I love to watch Practical Magic with a bottle of Apothic Red.[7] Ordering out for dinner, having a hot bath, and visiting with close friends for a cackle or two are essential when self-care is the priority.

---

7 *Practical Magic*. Directed by Griffin Dunne. Los Angeles, CA: Village Roadshow Pictures, 1998.

Diwali

The Hindu Festival of Lights is a beautiful celebration of life. Following a lunar calendar it can fall somewhere in either October or November each year. It calls on the Goddess Lakshmi, Goddess of wealth, fortune, and prosperity, and on the Elephant God Ganesh, Lord of success, to bless homes, families, and communities. Diwali also marks the victory of good over evil. We like to make colourful flags to hang in our doorways, lighting candles throughout the house and spending time with friends on this holiday.

Graveyard Visiting

Our family starts the New Year with an annual visit to a graveyard. We bring a picnic and offerings of biscuits, cookies, and nuts (things we know the squirrels and birds will enjoy), and we bring garbage bags to do a cleanup while we are there. We visit the graves and call out the names. We read all the epitaphs and try to imagine the people buried there, what were their stories, and how old they were when they died. A great exercise for building story-telling skills, we pick our favourite headstones and share our reasons with each other. This positive time spent in the graveyard will create lasting effects on you and your children, for it brings light to a place we have only associated with darkness. It helps demystify the graveyard and gives our children an opportunity to explore death and what it looks like without being thrust into it suddenly.

The more we can do to help ourselves, each other, and our children create safe places to talk about death, the more we promote a deep appreciation and respect for the cycle of life and death and how we can experience it.

The Mourning Moon

This month's full moon gives us the opportunity to embody our grief, to be fully in it, to allow the richness of our emotions to be honoured and expressed. This full moon gives you permission to have a good cry. When you look at it, remember your loved ones who have passed on, allow their memories to wash over you in this moonlight, bask in the fullness of the experience of them and the impact they had on you.

Take a moment to write their names here and note something special about each one.

KRISTA THORNHILL

A Place for Your Thoughts

A Place for Your Thoughts

DECEMBER: CELEBRATE

Element of Air

Christmas Stories, by Krista Thornhill, 2015

For the Earth Table: holly, white candles, angels, nativity scene, images of the sun, and cards of thanksgiving.

December: Celebrate

THE INTERNAL JOURNEY

The Birth of Hope

December calls us to find hope in the darkness. We celebrate and give thanks for the natural law and order of the Earth; that in the darkest soil a seed will begin to sprout, that in the darkness of the womb a life can be conceived, that in the darkest times of our lives we are truly being re-birthed.

From Solstice onwards, the sun will begin its return and stay longer and longer in the sky. Some cultures celebrate this beautiful time with the birth of the Christ Child, following a star in the sky. As we get geared up for Christmas, ponder what it is that makes this holiday so exciting. Consider too, what the Earth is doing -she is getting ready to come back to life! For this, we should be really excited!

If it is hard in all of the commercialization to stay focused on what it's all about-that we are celebrating hope- take comfort in knowing that no matter what our circumstances, we can have hope and joy in the fact that the darkness does not prevail.

The overwhelming pressure to make Christmas happen for everyone can be a huge distraction from the simplicity of the Christmas message:

there is light in the darkness! This month is all about connecting to the Earth as she prepares to give birth once again. As we approach the longest night of the year, explore ways to keep your celebrations simple and on point.

The Divine Feminine

Early Earth followers celebrated this time of year by honouring the Divine Feminine. It was the time of the Night Mother, she who laboured throughout the night to give birth to the sun. Many gods and goddesses have been honoured throughout civilization at this great time of birthing. Amaterasu, the Japanese Goddess of the Sun is a Goddess who was born at this time. The Norse Goddess Freya gave birth to Baldur, the Sun, and the Egyptian Goddess Isis gave birth to Horus, the Sun. The Christian Mary gave birth to Jesus Christ and the birth of Sarasvati, the Hindu Goddess of knowledge and the Queen of Heaven, is celebrated during Yuletide.

These Ancestral Mothers hold the spark of truth as they lead us through the dark labouring of our lives. They remind us that we are a part of something wonderful -the birthing of something new and promising and that the pains of labour are well worth it.

Before we get swallowed up in the festivities, let us take a moment to ground,[8] centre[9] and find our truth.[10] Where do we go overboard? What stresses us the most about the holiday? What would we change? And never mind everyone else, how would we truly like to celebrate this

---

8   ground: to find our footing mentally, emotionally and spiritually; to feel balanced, rooted and unbiased

9 centre: to find and hold calm focus

10 find our truth: what feels right for us

holiday? By answering these questions, we are honouring the feminine within us -men and women alike. By taking care of ourselves, loving ourselves and even being selfish, we are in our feminine consciousness. This holiday, treat yourself by making time for a special drink at your favourite place, buying that one thing you've been hoping someone would give you, or take yourself to the spa. In the taking care of everyone else, make time for you!

THE EXTERNAL JOURNEY

Winter Solstice: December 21-22nd

We honour the longest night of the year with the burning of the Yule Log,[11] lit before the sun went down and watched throughout the long night until the sun returns in the morning. Mythically, pagans celebrate this as the time in which the Earth labours and gives birth once more to the sun. We give each other Solstice gifts, often new pajamas and a game for the family, and we gather with friends for a feast. We decorate our home with holly and cedar branches and light white candles on our Earth Table.

The Crèche

Traditionally, most of us have grown up in Christian environments and will think having a nativity scene on the Earth Table a little out of place when it comes to pagan celebrations, but as it was explained to me years ago, it's quite symbolically accurate and beautiful. If we understand that this season celebrates the rebirth of the sun, then we

---

11 Yule Log: a specially selected log burnt on a hearth as a Christmas tradition

can value the symbolism of the birth story, of a baby as it represents the birth of the infant sun.

This idea of a crèche is made beautiful when you invite young children to bring their favourite toys to make up the crèche. One year my sister and I made a whole nativity scene on the mantel piece with our Barbies. Have the young ones pick out which toys will represent the characters of the story, deciding which doll will be the baby sun, and let them create the crèche. There are beautiful stories to tell as they do this. One story is "The Rebirth of the Sun" by Starhawk, found in one of her first books, *Circle Round: Raising Children in the Goddess Tradition*.[12] It's a book I recommend to everyone who has young children in their lives.

Planting Hope

Our favourite tradition, usually done at our Yule celebration but can be done anytime in December, is bulb planting. We give the children terra cotta pots to decorate and give them soil and a bulb to plant in their pot. It's is a beautiful way to teach children that life needs darkness to be birthed, and it needs their love and nurturing to grow. As they water and watch the bulb grow and burst forth from the soil, so they learn how to trust that the Earth does deliver; out from the darkness, a beautiful form of life springs forth. Over the following months, they will get to watch their flower grow, and come spring, will be able to take it outside and transfer into the ground if they choose. It is an act of letting go and releasing, just like their parents will have to do with them when they grow up. It is a lovely way to teach love, trust, and hope and makes a wonderful gift.

---

12 Starhawk, Diane Baker and Anne Hill, "The Rebirth of the Sun," in *Circle Round: Raising Children in the Goddess Tradition* (New York: Bantam Books, 1998), 98.

The Long Nights Moon

The last full moon of the year is a time to fill up on all of your gratitude for all that the year has brought you, the joys: the sufferings, the learnings, the challenges, and the breakthroughs. As we move closer to the darkest night of the year, use this full moonlight to kindle hope in the darkness. Take a moonlit walk and while moon gazing, let your heart fill with the hope of new birth. This moons mantra, "I am full of new beginnings!"

Use the space on this page to document some of the things you are grateful for that this past year has brought your way.

A Place for Your Thoughts

JANUARY: INTENTION

Element of Fire

Smudging the Garden, by Krista Thornhill, 2017

For the Earth Table: matches, wishes in written form, red candles, and incense

January: Intention

Living mostly in urban places, we have lost the appreciation for the power of fire. No longer needing it to heat our homes or cook our food, we are lucky if we can find a place to have an outside fire pit where we can share the evening with friends. For most of us, fire is a great threat that could take out neighborhoods, apartment buildings, and forests. Fire is a greatly feared and destructive force that shows no mercy, no bias. The next three months we will look at how to harness and use the element of Fire as a productive and healing force as we connect with the Earth in all her elements.

THE INTERNAL JOURNEY

Courage

> *Courage is not the absence of fear; it is the making of action in spite of fear, the moving out against resistance engendered by fear into the unknown and into the future.*
>
> *The Road Less Travelled* – Scott M. Peck

It takes great courage to stand and face the Fire because in truth we can never know the outcome. Looking back through our story and into the stories of our parents and grandparents takes courage; we don't always know what we will find there, so we must allow ourselves to be ignited by curiosity and by the desire to create healing in our lives. This takes a courageous heart.

What things have bothered you while hibernating inside or over the holidays, spending time with family and friends? What came up for you? Did you lose your temper over something or someone? Did you get too stressed out and become overwhelmed? Did you learn something from your past that needs to be released and healed? Look with courage and with the intention to find answers.

January calls us to reflect seriously about what is bothering us and asks us to look honestly at why we are allowing these things to control us. It asks us to examine the influences that the past has had on us: what elements of the story have been passed on from generation to generation? What needs healing and a change of action?

Working with the element of Fire, ask yourself, "What am I afraid of?" Now is the time to think about your fears. What do you need to do to find the courage to take control of and create change in your life?

This is what we bring to the fire as our offerings, the things we are now capable of seeing and acknowledging. We ask the destructive forces of Fire to burn away what no longer serves us.

Write these things on paper (or on bay leaves) and let them burn as a symbol of your intention to create change for this New Year.

THE EXTERNAL JOURNEY

The Power of Fire

As we move into the South, let us not fear Fire but look for its comfort. I take the visual of Sam McGee,[13] the gold miner from Tennessee, finally comfortable in the heat of the fire, and I cannot help but be challenged to find my own comfort in the heat of the flames. In this cold season of the year, we come back to the Fire. This month, we return to our primal roots, we draw nearer to the flame, and we let our bodies absorb its heat. We take the time to sit and reflect around its brilliant destruction, we let the colours dance upon our skin, and we let go as it burns, devouring all that we no longer desire and that which makes us heavy.

This month, commit to making time for fires! This is how we harness the element to aid us. Call out the powers of Agni[14] and Oya[15] around your fire and ask them to show you what needs sacrificing for you to be transformed, delivered out of your darkness and into your light. Make time to watch the flames and allow your mind to get lost in them. This is what is called *fire scrying*, to allow the light and heat of the flames to inspire your vision for the future.

Spell Work

Anyone can spell. It is the act of writing down on paper your intention; what you want and what you will have to do to make it happen. It's about accepting responsibility for creating what you want. January thus

13   Robert W. Service, "The Cremation of Sam McGee," Poetry Foundation, accessed May 15, 2017, https://www.poetryfoundation.org/poems-and-poets/poems/detail/45081.

14   Agni: the Rig Vedic deity of fire and the conveyor of sacrifices to the Gods. He is also a God of divine knowledge, who leads man to the Gods. He was one of the most important of the Vedic Gods.

15   Oya: African Yoruba Tribal Goddess of fire, wind and thunder

is the perfect month for spell work. Begin by writing out intentions for the year, making them specific and detailed, and then gather your thoughts: what will you need to carry out these intentions?

A grocery list is a perfect example of how spelling works. You want to make something special, so you write out your grocery list based on the ingredients you need. You then go on an adventure to the grocery store or the market to obtain the things on your list. Everything you encounter along the way adds magic to what you are doing. Once home, you begin putting the ingredients together, and you create and serve your meal. Write down everything you want and be as specific as possible. The writing down is an essential element as it acts as a contract between yourself (your brain) and the universe.

Spelling sets the mind to action. Knowing that the brain believes what you tell it and that every idea begins with the brain, spelling is a specific way to literally *spell it out* for your brain so that it can act on manifesting that which you wish to have happen and in the way you wish it to be. And like every to do list, remember to leave room for the unexpected.

To really convince the brain of what you want, use all five senses to help it understand your intentions. For example, we wanted to move from Alberta to BC and to do this we needed our house to sell for what we were asking for and no less. For sound, I played whale music and sounds of the ocean, for taste I imported blackberries and apples, for touch I had sea shells, for sight I had pictures of my favourite forest places, and for smell I burned cedar smudges. I took a whole month to focus on this intention, and as a result, our house sold for exactly what we wanted!

Spell when you are taking responsibility for what you want to manifest, pray when you need help making it happen, and allow for the universe to bring it to pass as it will.

Smudging

An ancient spiritual practice found in many different religions around the world is smudging, the use of smoke as a cleansing agent. Smudging is a Shamanic tool using all the elements of the Earth. A stick of dried herbs representing Earth is lit with Fire to create smoke. Held in one hand, a shell is most commonly used to collect the ashes of the smudge, the shell representing Water. Using a feather, representing Air, the smudge is fanned to keep the smudge smouldering.

Perform a smudge before a ceremony or special gathering to not only get rid of negative energy but to invite blessings upon an individual or space.

Smudging is used to cleanse and clear; to wash away impurities, sadness, anxiety, dark thoughts or unwanted energies and to evoke generosity, appreciation, wisdom, praise, and gratitude. You can make your own smudge or purchase one; sweet grass, sage, rosemary, and lavender are the most commonly used plants.

The Cold Wolf Moon

This month's full moon calls us to defy the darkness, to be bold and courageous like the wolf. It's a time to step outdoors and into your fullness to howl! Be as loud as you can, wake the neighbours, frighten little children, stir your soul and claim your power in the moonlight. For you are voracious, a force to be reckoned with! You are not afraid of the dark! You are powerful, mighty, and divine! Howl!

A Place for Your Thoughts

FEBRUARY: LOVE

Element of Fire

Unconditional, by Krista Thornhill, 2016

For the Earth Table: hearts, lace, pink candles, primroses and old Valentine's cards

February: Love

All friend feelings for others are an extension of a man's feelings for himself.

- Aristotle, *Ethics*

After spending the month of January delving into our darkness, scrying into the Fires to seek revelation and to build courage, we need a little loving. January's Fire is destructive and burns away the debris from our lives, but in doing so, also creates space for new life to grow. February we look at the hot, steamy and passionate elements of fire. This month we turn our focus towards love in all of its beautiful forms, including Agape[16] and Eros.[17] February calls us to love ourselves in this process of refinement and purification, to extend grace and mercy to ourselves and to those who are close and important to us. It's a time to show compassion and empathy to all of those around us. For this is truly the change we need to be a part of in making our world a safer and more welcoming place for all. This month, seek new inspiration and hope for the future.

---

16 Agape: Greek; goodwill, benevolence, and willful delight as the object of love

17 Eros: Greek; intimate or romantic love

THE INTERNAL JOURNEY

Inspiration

Contemplate who it is that inspires you. Reflect on the people who have had positive influences in your life. What hurdles did they have to face or what obstacles did they have to overcome? What has been the key to their success? How have they made it this far?

Inspiration can be used as an amazing motivator to get us moving toward our goals. It's a powerful tool to have in your tool belt at this time of year, when darkness lingers and when we're feeling low in energy and spirit. What are your life goals? What are the things on your bucket list? Imagine what these inspiring people would say or do to give you encouragement and support.

Write your answers down and ponder over them. If you have the opportunity, make an effort to let these people know that they have had a positive effect on you and have been a source of inspiration to you.

Take this month as an opportunity to thank the people that have inspired you. Write them a letter, call them on the phone or message them any way you can to let them know that they had an impact on your life. Use the rest of this page to jot down a few people who have inspired you.

THE EXTERNAL JOURNEY

Imbolc[18] and the Goddess Brigit[19]

This is an ancient Gaelic holiday celebrated on February first and second, commemorating and aligning with the first signs of spring. At this time, pagans celebrate the Celtic Goddess Brigit, also known as St. Brigit by Catholics. She is the Goddess of Fire, inspiration, poetry, smith-work and fertility. Brigit, also known as Bride, Bridey, Brighid, Briggidda, Brigantia, was known for her compassion and goodness. Celtic myth attributes these characteristics to have brought peace and unity to the warring Celtic tribes of her time. Revered throughout Celtic history and preserved by the Roman Catholic Church, St. Brigit is still recognized today during the religious celebration of Candlemas,[20] where you will see St. Brigit crosses made out of tall river grass and displayed over doorways as a sign of protection against fire.

This is a great holiday to participate in, especially if you need some help kick-starting your intentions for the New Year. Bring them written on paper and offer them to the Imbolc fires, for this is the celebration of beginnings, the time for initiation![21]

---

18 Imbolc: Celtic celebration of the first signs of spring, when the sheep are pregnant; a time for new beginnings

19 Goddess Brigit: Celtic triple goddess ruling healing, poetry, and smith-craft; one of the great mothers of the Celts; also adopted by the Roman Catholic Church as St. Brigid

20 Candlemas: a Christian holiday celebrated annually on February 2; celebrates three occasions according to Christian belief: the presentation of the child Jesus, Jesus' first entry into the temple, and the Virgin Mary's purification

21 initiation: the action of beginning something

Love

Love is a conscious act, not the warm fuzzies you feel when enamoured with someone. Though love can take many forms (Agape, Eros, Philia[22], and Storge[23]) love is a choice for a parent, friend, or lover. Love is a choice because it must be decided upon and because it requires, in all forms, consideration for another. Love is an act we share and an expensive gift we give, for it comes at the cost of self, of putting someone else first.

Self-love requires putting ourselves first, putting our highest good before our ego. Making hard decisions for ourselves is never easy when the ego wants what it wants. Ego is the young lover who wants attention, the addict who wants just one more hit; the prideful parent who can't let go for the sake of winning an argument. The ego wants the quick and easy path to gratification. Loving ourselves first can mean having to deny the ego and create healthy boundaries for ourselves, out of love for self. It's not easy work, but we must believe we are worthy of it and deserving of it if we are to ever share our love with someone else.

Love for others can only be truly shared when we know what it means to love ourselves first. For to "do unto others as you would have them do unto you" means nothing if we don't first love ourselves.[24]

This month, how can you celebrate with the Earth as she loves herself? She is tender and quiet as she nurses her newborn. She is in no hurry to reveal what she is creating; fruits of her labour still lay underground, incubating, developing. How can you relate this to your intentions

22 Philia: Greek; friendship as a kind of love

23 Storge: Greek; parental love for a child, the love between family members

24 Mt 7:12

for the New Year? In what areas can you slow down and love yourself first before you show the world what you're up to? February is incubation time.

The Quickening Moon

This full moon puts a spring in our step and wind in our sails, for it is a motivating moon. This is a good moon for making plans, deciding on actions, and moving forward on a project. Being the month of Initiation and new beginnings, we are aligning with the Earth as she too nurses new life in the darkness of the soil. We are getting closer to spring every day! Check in with this moon while it's full, even if it means just stopping for a moment at the window before bed. Stop, stare and as you moon gaze, take deep slow breaths, and with every inhale, imagine you are taking into your lungs the Earth's power to grow things in darkness.

Feel that power filling your lungs and at that moment agree with yourself, "Yes! I can!"

A Place for Your Thoughts

MARCH: CREATIVE MADNESS

Element of Fire

Shells & Broken Glass, by Krista Thornhill, 2017

For the Earth Table: rabbits, clover, sprouting bulbs, tea cups, ribbons, and candles

March: Creative Madness

This is the month of cabin fever madness, fire in its most wild and unpredictable form! As the Earth herself becomes schizophrenic, being in neither spring nor winter, this is the month where we are allowed by natural order to go a little crazy. Remembering to love ourselves in this place of in-between, this is the time to do unexpected things, to push our boundaries, to go a little mad as we consider the March Hare, and to trust that at the end of the month balance shall be restored with the Spring Equinox. [25] This, for me, is the last month dedicated to indoor projects and the time for a deep spring clean, for soon the warm weather will start to pull and no matter where we are with those indoor projects, it's time to focus on completing them or putting them away. For as the light begins to call us out from our hibernations, it is soon time to turn our attention to the outdoor things that we like doing.

THE INTERNAL JOURNEY

Sunday, MARCH 23, 2014: ARTICLES OF MADNESS. #7 EAGLES ARE ASSHOLES. JUST SAYING. - Indira A. Ravynmoon, *unpublished writing*

---

25 March Hare: of the rabbit family, herbivorous and long-eared, they are fast runners and they typically live solitarily or in pairs

Unbridled Creativity

Do something different this month to push your comfort zones; encourage yourself to do something wild, out of character, perhaps even unpredictable, and choose to blame it entirely on the weather! This month let out your crazy; I dare you! One night at a pub in March, I once told a police officer that I thought he was the stripper we had ordered. He blushed and left quickly from the back deck where we were partying! Celebrate your madness and what makes you unique and special, flaunt it, and be unbridled and uncensored this month!

The March Hare

In a fit of cabin fever, I went looking for meaning in my madness and felt incredibly attracted to the idea of studying the March Hare. Within my research, I discovered that unlike other rabbits, the hare is nocturnal and lives alone year round. Mating season brings the hare out of isolation and forces it to socialize with others. In being thrust into mating, and with the rush of hormones that comes with it, the hare acts unpredictably, erratically, and often violently. Did you know that a pregnant hare can conceive a second time while already pregnant? This makes me laugh! I can relate to this crazed image of the March Hare. Forever now, the hare will be my mascot for this month, so let out your crazy, be erratic, be dynamic and, if necessary, fight back!

THE EXTERNAL JOURNEY

Holi: Festival of Colours

This beautiful Hindu Holiday is a spring festival held in early March in India and Nepal. Celebrating the return of the light in its myriad of colours, neighborhoods erupt into the streets in India this month, dousing each other in bright coloured paint powder as a way to welcome and celebrate each other as community members, symbolizing their togetherness. What a fitting celebration for creative madness, an explosion of colours!

Spring Equinox: Ostara

The return of balance on March 21st, where night meets day on equal ground, is a celebration that marks the beginning of spring. Ostara, the Germanic Goddess of dawn, fertility, and spring, is celebrated on the equinox. [26] Eggs, seeds, and newborn animals represent themes of rebirth marking the time where life and death are in balance with each other. Now is the time to plant seeds, turn soil, and prepare gardens. It's the time to welcome spring by doing a deep cleaning and by washing floors and windows.

The Worm Moon

Fitting for this month, is its Algonquin name, known by other cultures as Full Crow or Full Sap, the Worm Moon acknowledges the return of animals and natural resources after a long winter's sleep. Considered the last moon of winter, the worm represent regeneration, its ability to survive by digging deep into the darkness only to rise again when

---

26 Ostara: Celtic celebration of the spring equinox and Germanic goddess of spring

the ground warms. In your own rise out of winter, take this moment to acknowledge how far you've come! Do a little worm dance in the moonlight, have a wiggle and a giggle at how funny life can be. Moon Mantra, "I am hilarious!"

A Place for Your Thoughts

.

A Place for Your Thoughts

APRIL: REBIRTH

Element of Water

Beach Treasure, by Krista Thornhill, 2017

For the Earth Table: water, sea shells, blue/white candles, chalice, fresh flowers, pictures of jesters (The Fool tarot card), circus paraphernalia, juggling balls, dice.

April: Rebirth

Oh the element of Water, washing away all the dust, smoke and the chill of winter from our bodies! I am so ready to plunge myself into water, so ready for Spring! No matter where we live, April never ceases to fail in its delivery. It always manages to give us those glimpses of hope fulfilled, of a promise delivered, of faith manifested. We are witness to the great miracle of life; Spring following Winter! Consistently She never fails us, Gaia always makes way for Spring!

THE INTERNAL JOURNEY

Stop taking yourself so seriously and come get in the Water! April always brings up my insecurities as it calls me out of my craziness and asks me to lighten up. In this light, I find myself questioning my sense of self-worth because I honestly do crazy very well. March is a fun month of catering to the madness of my mind, but it does make me question my mental health, which is just what this month is supposed to do! I call it my Mental Health Month, but after being in it for so long, I definitely feel a little vulnerable and insecure. April calls me to "come out and play, already!"

But what if my madness doesn't settle into some kind of operational normalcy? What if no one will understand me and think I'm nuts?

What if I push myself too far and can't come back? This is the darkness of my Self, my shadows, the place where thoughts are not always of a shareable kind, where I would not want to be seen by others, where I can easily scare myself. April calls me out from this dark madness of my mind and says "come play now and stop the ramblings of your mind." I find myself questioning my sanity, my worthiness, my inherent right for sound mindedness. April calls me to have no regard for mental conditioning; to let go of worry, fear, and anxiety; to rebirth myself; to come back to the innocence of my childhood; to just play.

The Earth prepares herself for transition, making herself vulnerable as new life begins to shoot forth and break soil. She begins to shed her winter garments, the things that kept her safe and warm, and now her shoulders are bare, her skin revealed, and she is beautifully exposed and tender in her maidenhood.

Worthiness

As we emerge from the comfort of our winter dens and out into the dewy grass and wet soil, our feet tingle, our hands get dirty, and our bodies sigh with relief to be outdoors again. With the buzz of spring in the air and summer on its way, we cannot help but make plans for holiday fun, outdoor projects, activities, and parties in the park...yet deep down inside something within us grieves for the comfort of the wood stove, the long dark nights, and the quiet of inside living. For some, the expectations of active living can stir up feelings of unworthiness. I feel this every season, for as I find myself getting more and more excited about the lifestyle change that this season brings, the shadows of the Underworld pull at my lifting spirit, trying to keep me down. Fight for it! Draw ever upwards! Allow yourself to be fully resurrected from your darkness and claim yourself worthy of the spring, the summer of all things, of love and light.

The Fool

Until you are ready to look foolish, you'll never have the possibility of being great!

– Cher

Fool's day starts the month off with trickery and jest. We come out of our fortress-like boundaries, push through our madness, and tumble out into playtime. In the Tarot deck, the Fool is numbered zero, representing the unlimited potential that is at the start of every journey. It is the card to mark new beginnings and to venture forth with a child-like heart. Now is the time to connect with your inner child: the believer in dreams, the fearless and courageous self, and the innocent and playful parts of ourselves.[27]

THE EXTERNAL JOURNEY
April Showers Bring May Flowers

This month pay extra attention to the weather. One of the major causes of the often heavy downpours is the position of the jet stream.[28] In early spring, the jet stream starts to move northwards, allowing large depressions to bring strong winds and rain in from the Ocean. In one day

---

27 inner child: in popular psychology and analytical psychology, inner child is our childlike aspect; includes all that we learned and experienced as children, before puberty

28 jet stream: like rivers of wind, high above in the atmosphere; slim strips of strong winds that have a huge influence on climate, as they can push air masses around and affect weather patterns

the weather can change from warming sunshine to sleet and snow. The track of these depressions can often bring bands of rain followed by heavy showers, even hail or snow and strong blustery winds.

As we align ourselves more and more with the changing season, we can allow ourselves more grace and ease as we too allow for personal jet streams to navigate through our lives. Not yet in full swing of spring, melting snow, slush and salt stains on our boots remind us of our own transitional streams and explains depressive mood swings. Take care of yourself this month and allow for downtime. This is the time of year not to be hard on yourself; when you catch yourself feeling down, blame it on April showers! If you didn't make time for your crazy in March, make sure to allot time for some foolishness this April.

The Art of Play

Feed your inner child and re-discover fun! When was the last time you had fun? Be conscious not to let work become your identity and your responsibilities define you. When was the last time you had a real belly laugh? What was the last thing you did that made you feel excited? These are important things for us to keep in mind, for it is these things that connect us to the joy of daffodils, bluebells, baby sheep, and the return of hummingbirds. Admittedly, I have kept my children's favourite toys, not because my children have asked me to but because their old toys help me stay connected to the part of me that enjoyed playing. The journey is full of ups and downs, trials and challenges, valleys and mountain tops, and if we don't remember to have fun, we end up taking life way too seriously. Enjoy the good times! Make time to play this month; you deserve it after a long winter. Do something special and fun outside to commemorate the changing of the season.

Alice in Wonderland: A Story of Descent and Resurrection

Lewis Carroll's children's story is a fantastic read for children at this time. Complete with bunnies, hats, and hearts, *Alice in Wonderland* is truly our modern day version of the death, descent, and resurrection story.[29]

Like the mythical stories of Persephone[30] and Demeter,[31] Inanna[32] and Ereshkigal,[33] and even the death and resurrection story of Jesus Christ, the message of decent to the Underworld has been with us throughout time. It symbolizes the need to embrace death of what no longer serves us, to face the temptations that hide in our shadows, to battle with our demons, and to return to our Upper Worlds stronger, revived, and victorious. Carroll's tale of a journey to the Underworld, the dark side of our soul, is a beautiful story that teaches us not to fear our shadows, for it is when we surrender and lay down all the things we cling to that we can make peace with our demons and conquer our fears.

Beauty in Vulnerability

It's time to put the long johns away! How are you feeling under all those layers? Vulnerable? Bare? Not ready to don a bathing suit and hit the lawn chair? Believe it or not, this is what is happening to the Earth

---

29 Carroll, "Alice in Wonderland," 13-47.

30 Persephone: Greek Goddess; the daughter of Zeus and the harvest Goddess Demeter and Queen of the underworld; abducted by the God Hades and then later saved by her mother

31 Demeter: Greek Goddess of agriculture, the earth and fertility

32 Inanna: Sumerian Goddess of fertility and war; engages in a yearly conflict with Ereshkigal in the underworld

33 Ereshkigal: Mesopotamian Goddess; Sumerian Queen of the underworld; also known as the "great below"

at this time; in her maiden days, she is young and ready to blossom, yet the safety of winter is not far from her mind, and she is vulnerable as she begins to take off her outer layers.

New shoots are pushing their way up through the soil, breaking ground, hoping not to be trampled on; animals are coming out of their dens looking for food; fruit trees are budding, and butterflies are taking first flight. It's a beautiful and fragile time. So if you are feeling vulnerable and fragile now, as I know I am, I am feeling wet-winged like a butterfly just out of its cocoon, know that this is exactly how you should be feeling.

Align with the Earth and find the beauty in your vulnerability; take extra care and protect yourself by not allowing fragility to become insecurity. This is the time to feed your inner child, return to innocence, take flight upon the warming winds, and be youthful. Embrace the Fool and take new steps, unencumbered by the weight of winter clothing. Don't second guess yourself or lose your sense of self- worth; you have earned this time to shine, so don't be afraid to do so.

Be gentle with yourself as you spread your wings and love your body as you lighten your wardrobe –it has kept you safe and warm all winter. Be gracious and compassionate with yourself, with others, and with the Earth. Take time to stop and notice the new buds, the early morning birdsong, the tubers breaking the soil, and be comforted and find rest in the knowing that this too shall pass. Make every effort to enjoy every moment to the fullest, for before we know it, we will be in the thrust of summer and this time of beautiful transition will be behind us.

The Pink Moon

Named so by the Native Americans, this month's moon honors the first blooms of the Cheery Tree and the Phlox, a rejuvenating dose of beauty and joy after a long bleak winter! This is the first full moon of spring, a wonderful reason to have a party! Make it a pink party! It's time for fun and what a better way to be in alignment with Gaia, as she pulls out her dress-up box and invites you to get silly with her. In the light of this moon declare, "I am glorious! I am magnificent! I am wonderful!"

A Place for Your Thoughts

A Place for Your Thoughts

A Place for Your Thoughts

MAY: PLEASURE

Element of Water

Sage & Lavender, by Krista Thornhill, 2016

For the Earth Table: crystals, amethysts, fresh flowers, purple/blue candles, lavender

May: Pleasure

The first blooms are so very welcomed, as my garden explodes with irises. We welcome this month with the fertility rite of Beltane when Celtic families would bring their livestock to the ritual bonfires to be blessed by its smoke, where celebrations would last for days reveling in the sexual energy of the season and invoking blessings from the gods for good and fruitful crops.

Gaia the young maiden dons her white dress and puts flowers in hair, she dances barefoot in the grass. Her breasts are perky and her skin fair, she smells of vanilla leaves, she is innocent and fertile. She blushes at the sight and smell of him, the young Sun God, the stag, as he approaches her and like a young school girl, she drops her gaze and smiles. There is nothing but the two of them: ripe for each other, there is no one or no creature to cause them shame or hesitation as they playfully chase each other, tugging and teasing. With their lovemaking, her belly grows full of life. This is their courtship: the natural, unadulterated play of the maiden and the God.

THE INTERNAL JOURNEY

The Sacral Chakra[34]

The Sacral Chakra, found in the pelvic area, represents our interactions with others: with acquaintances, friends, family members, and lovers. It is in this place in the body where we hold our experiences of trust and our innate desire to create. Thus it is in this place where our sexuality is activated. Associated with the element of Water, our sacral chakra is the well of our emotions. It is here, in our bodies, where we store the history of our sexual experiences and explore our self-worth in our most intimate of relations. When the sacral chakra is balanced within us, it enables us to truly trust and relax in intimate situations. Healing work with this part of our body creates the ability to both give and receive fully, to show up fully present, self-loving, emotionally-balanced, and truly authentic.

Say *Yes!*

Nothing brings out the inner child more than being open to new adventures! Reconnect with your younger self and with what gives you pleasure. When was the last time you did something you were passionate about?

Each May, I make a conscious decision to say yes! Yes to me! Yes to every opportunity that presents itself to me, appeals to my curiosity, and provides a sense of pleasure. As a result, I have gone on fabulous adventures, discovering passions that have been forgotten, put on the

---

34 Chakra system: Chakra, meaning 'wheel' in Sanskrit; seven chakras points in our bodies in which energy flows through; blocked energy in our seven chakras can often lead to illness, so it's important to understand what each chakra represents and what we can do to keep this energy flowing freely

back burner, or needed instigating. This yearly exercise challenges me to trust that the energy I am putting out into the world is what I will attract back to myself. It calls me to pay attention to how quickly I am accustomed to saying no, even to the things I really want, and how quickly I dismiss opportunities for my own pleasure because of cost, time restraints, children... The list of excuses can be long.

THE EXTERNAL JOURNEY

Beltane: May First

Beltane is a Gaelic holiday celebrating the fertility of the Earth at the halfway point between the spring equinox and the summer solstice.[35] It is also known as *balefire*. Traditionally, the farming communities kept their animals close to home in the winter months, often living with their animals. Before sending the animal out to the fields to graze for the spring and summer months, the farmers would build huge bonfires up on the hills on the way out of the village. The smoke from these fires would help rid the animals of ticks and lice before being set loose on the hillside.

The changing season was always an opportunity for celebration, not only would they make a grand procession through the village with their animals, but the farmers' daughters would also participate in a contest to see who would be chosen as the May Queen. This event would celebrate fertility, often lasting for three days: feasting, dancing, playing music, and even pursuing sexual exploits were encouraged to increase the fertility of the village.

---

35 Beltane: the Anglicized name for the Gaelic May Day festival

The Maypole

The Maypole[36] is erected in celebration of the union of the Divine Masculine[37] and the Divine Feminine.[38] Traditionally, the morning after the balefire, young and old alike would come out of the bushes from their night of frolic and gather around the pole, taking ribbons in hand. As men would move one way and women the other, they would begin dancing around the pole, weaving the ribbons together as they danced, weaving over and below each other, getting closer and closer until the entire pole was wrapped tightly in a colourful display of ribbons, the participants face to face.

The Flower Moon

Celebrating the return of the blossoms, this is a beautiful time to honor yourself with the gift of flowers, or someone else. Create a flower pedal mandala, a flower crown or just adorn your home with a beautiful bouquet to celebrate the beauty of this life! This moons mantra is, "I am beautiful! I am open! I am free to express myself!"

---

36 Maypole: a tall, wooden pole erected as a part of various European folk festivals, around which a maypole dance often took place; inserting the pole into the Earth is symbolic of intercourse and the dance of weaving the ribbons together is a celebration of the sacred marriage of the masculine and the feminine

37 Divine Masculine: represents a spiritual, psychological, archetypal ideal-the best and most inspiring, elevating, and restorative aspects of masculine expression and manifestation in the universe; the energy of the masculine is direct, active, goal orientated, driven and to the point

38 The Divine Feminine: represents the supreme level of feminine expression and manifestation in the universe; the energy of the feminine is creative, expansive, restorative, compassionate, and healing.

A Place for Your Thoughts

A Place for Your Thoughts

JUNE: ENGAGE

Element of Water

Hide and Seek Frog, by Krista Thornhill, 2016

For the Earth Table: yellow candles, flowers, stones from the garden

June: Engage

June feels very grounding to me as if I have arrived after a very long journey and now feel firmly planted. June is a perfect month: everything is easier and I feel like I can get a lot done. It's warm and dry outside, making it easier to expand. Expanding my lifestyle, we cook outside on the barbecue, I hang laundry on the line to dry, I tend to the garden, I pack picnics for outdoor destinations, and I retreat to the lawn chair instead of the couch. It's a summer month, yet with the routine of school, it still has structure, and it's that very thing that makes it so enjoyable for me. There's a sense of hope and excitement in the air, and I feel accomplished and focused.

The Earth is now hard at work alongside her lover, the Sun, for they are tending the garden, her belly swelling with life. Not yet a time for frolicking in the fields, they turn their minds to working together as a team to get the jobs done. The Sun is the strong young man who drives the plough across the fields, and as his strength adds to hers, together they are a powerful team. Their union is as beautiful as it should be and they complement each other in their differences like all young lovers do. They are the marriage of all possibilities.

THE INTERNAL JOURNEY

Down and Dirty

When we make bold decisions and act big, there are bound to be repercussions to the same degree. For someone who doesn't like a particular change or a circumstance spurred on by miscommunication or a lack of understanding, change can bring out the worst in people. But this is the time to press on; no one is going to applaud our huge effort to step boldly forward, and no grand stage will appear for our regal bow, for the work is only just beginning.

When we get over our insecurities and step into the month of May, we must truly remain on the side of risk, stand in our power, radiate our glory, and persist on into June. Now is when the real work starts of applying ourselves, of doing the work. There is no garden that does not need weeding or plant that does not need watering. Keep in mind that we also need constant care and nourishing support. Do whatever necessary to take care of yourself this month. You are important!

In June, the sunflower stretches even taller; the oak arrives late and turns green; the pumpkin vine climbs out of the compost pile; and the nasturtiums stretch out, not bothered by the irises or the magnolia whose time for blooming is over – they are all doing their own thing regardless of what the other plants may be doing.

Though we may be called down, unfairly treated, betrayed, and even gossiped about, we stand in alignment with the Earth as she changes and we press on! We too must we get down and dirty with the work of being magnificent! Nothing worth having ever comes without effort!

June calls us to engage with her energy fully, to stay focused and committed. Now that we're out there, we should not shy away from the first challenge that arises! Don't wilt when things get hot! Dig deeper, push on, stand stronger, keep smiling! Do the work!

Come Summer Solstice, we will all really have something to celebrate! Don't be afraid to get down and dirty this month, for this is just exactly what the Earth herself is doing!

THE EXTERNAL JOURNEY

Summer Solstice: June 21-22

Honouring the longest day and the shortest night of the year, Litha is an ancient solar celebration.[39] This is when the power of the sun and the fertility of the earth are at their peaks.

The solstice, a Latin word meaning *sun stands still*, is a phenomenal moment in the year that has been celebrated throughout history. Midsummer, popularized by Shakespeare's "A Midsummer Night's Dream," was celebrated with hilltop bonfires, live music, and dancing.[40] It was a time to honour the space between the Earth and the Heavens and the relationship between Fire and Water. Some ancient cultures would celebrate Litha by setting a wagon wheel on fire and rolling it down a hill towards a body of water, representing the symbiotic relationship between the two elements.

---

39 Litha: the pagan celebration of Midsummer, also known as St. John's Day

40 William Shakespeare, "A Midsummer Night's Dream," in William Shakespeare: The Complete Works (New York: Barnes & Nobel, Inc., 1994), 279-301.

Celebrate Litha by answering the call to be outside. Spend the evening outdoors with a bonfire, live music, dancing circle, and barbecue with friends; sleep outside under the stars and light floating candles; stay up all night to cheer on the sun when it rises, or celebrate with a special early breakfast with friends.

Water Rituals

Water quenches thirst, puts out fire, and soothes the body.

All religions of the world have a significant use for Water in their rituals.[41] Water represents the rebirthing process of the spirit within the individual. Buddhism uses a water-pouring ritual for their funeral services. Believed to have spiritual cleansing powers as well as physical cleansing abilities, water fountains are commonly found in many of the world's religious centers, including Islam, Christianity, Hinduism, and Shintoism, wherein each it is encouraged that anyone entering the sacred inner temples is cleansed of all impurities. In the Western world, we are most familiar with Baptism within the Christian church, be it by full immersion or by sprinkling water on the forehead.

At least once this month, try to make it to a large enough body of water in which you can fully immerse yourself. Make this an opportunity to symbolically wash away the stains of winter and allow the healing nature of Water to revive your soul. Leave the water feeling renewed and restored.

---

41 sacred bath: Shamans in Ecuador perform a soul-cleansing ritual at Peguche Falls during the Ini Raymi fiesta, an ancient Incan celebration of the sun; believed that water gives a person power to work and the courage to dance for the fiesta

The Strawberry Moon

Also called the Honey Moon in Europe, celebrated with the drinking of mead, the Strawberry moon marks the beginning of harvest. Usually falling around Father's Day, it's a great way to celebrate the Solstice by adding strawberry's to everything. In the light of this moon declare, "I am delicious!

A Place for Your Thoughts

KRISTA THORNHILL

A Place for Your Thoughts

A Place for Your Thoughts

JULY: HAPPINESS

Element of Earth

Pink Roses from My Daughter, by Krista Thornhill, 2016

For the Earth Table: fresh fruits, beach shells, flowers, things that make you happy

July: Happiness

Take away the structure of school, and you have this sense of unlimited freedom; this expansion feels incredibly liberating and makes time seem to last forever. It's the time for festivals and late nights. The beautiful weather makes things feel effortless and more enjoyable. In this month, let go of the need for structure and routine and embrace a slower speed. Things will get done when they will and in the meantime, enjoy the flowers that are blooming and get to the water!

THE INTERNAL JOURNEY

Knowing

For the past two thousand years of human development, a lot of focus was put on the word *belief*.[42] Think of religion and its influence on society and how it has evolved. Consider how beliefs have become the largest division between us, how we have used beliefs to define ourselves and our cultures. Belief has been the fuel for judgment, division, and hate. Belief has been the stronghold that has kept us distracted from knowing –it has kept us in ignorance.

---

42 belief: a feeling of being sure that someone of something exists or that something is true; the state of mind in which a person thinks something to be the case, with or without there being empirical evidence to prove that something is the case with factual certainty

The Age of Aquarius,[43] which is happening now, calls us to focus on the word *know*.[44] Even the Bible said that people would die from the rejection of knowledge.[45] We have seen the evidence of this all over the globe and throughout history as we know it, for where a lack of knowledge exists, children starve, wars rage, young people get addicted, sexually transmitted infections spread, domestic violence is prevalent, and religions are radical.

The time has passed when feeling sure of something or accepting the truth will suffice. If there is to be a change in the world and change in our lives, it must begin with acquiring knowledge by whatever means possible. It's time not to believe the truth, but to *know* the truth.[46]

To know the truth one must be able to accept and be present in every situation without judgment, allowing for things to be as they are, without expectation and alteration. To know the truth is to be at peace with the world.

When we live a life connected to the Earth's cycles, we *know* that the seasons will follow each other. This simple truth gives incredible peace if we allow for it.

This month we ask ourselves, *what am I certain of? What am I knowledgeable about? What do I know?* As we apply our learning, let us stand in our knowledge and know ourselves to be true! This is the power we must harness at this time in history, now more than ever!

---

43 Age of Aquarius: an astrological term denoting either the current or forthcoming astrological age

44 know: to perceive or understand as fact or truth; to apprehend clearly and with certainty

45 Hos 4:6

46 true: being in accordance with the actual state of affairs; consistent, steadfast, loyal, honest and just

Happiness

Happy people are motivated, creative, and productive.-
Stefan Goldfinch, *The 7 Habits of Happy People*

I think we have been greatly misled to believe that happiness is something we achieve *at the end* of action; I am learning that happiness is found *in* action.

Happy is a state of flow, where you experience peace and joy in the present moment. July is a perfect time for finding peace and joy in your moments! The weather is warm, Earth has her party dress on, and every weekend is a long one! July is all about being happy. Find tasks that you enjoy, that you can lose yourself in, forget about your concerns and let go of time.

From my studies in positive psychology, I have learned that happy people have seven things in common. They value relationships and nurture the ones they are in. They are caring individuals who give of their time and share their gifts and strengths with others. They value their physical health and take care of their bodies, they exercise and eat healthily. They are spiritually conscious people and are open-minded and non-judgmental. They are generally positive and mindful people, observant of their environment, and patient and thoughtful of others. You will find them engaged in activities they enjoy and are good at, and most often you will be able to see their strengths and virtues being put to good use.[47]

---

47 "Positive Psychology and the Science of Happiness," Pursuit of Happiness, December 15, 2016, accessed May 23, 2017, http://www.pursuit-of-happiness.org/science-of-happiness/.

Happiness is a choice: a choice to be in the moment without complaint. "There are no problems," Eckhart Tolle says, "just challenges."[48] If we focus on our strengths, take care of our health, maintain healthy committed relationships with others, and nurture the Divine within ourselves, we can create flow in our lives on a daily basis. When we create flow, challenges become interesting bumps in the ride down the river.

THE EXTERNAL JOURNEY

Walking the Walk

It can't all be love and light if there's been no battle won in the shadows; it means nothing if we are not living examples of what we say we believe and hold true. I love this dictionary definition of walk: "moves at a regular and fairly slow pace by lifting and setting down each foot, in turn, never having both feet off the ground at once." Walking our walk is not about quick fixes, it's about taking our time to apply what we have learned. After all of the work we have done on ourselves, the self-help books we've read, the different healing modalities we've tried, and the great motivational speakers we've listened to and been inspired by, it's now time to apply all that we have learned. Don't do anything else this month but be in the present moment. Allow yourself to enjoy the fruits of your labour, bask in the glory of transformation as you see it happening in nature all around you, and give yourself permission to be on sabbatical. It is all for naught if we can't manifest it in our daily lives.

---

48 Eckhart Tolle, "The Power of Now" (speech, Vancouver, BC, April 16th, 2016).

The Blessing Moon

Also called the Full Buck Moon, in honor of the male bucks getting their antlers, and Thunder \moon to honour the thunderous summer skies of the Canadian Prairies, this moon calls for a full moon sleep over party! When we were children, with all the parents, we would make a big family bed the length of the back yard and together we'd all sleep under the stars. This moon calls us to take account of how blessed we are. Moon mantra, "I am blessed!"

A Place for Your Thoughts

KRISTA THORNHILL

A Place for Your Thoughts

A Place for Your Thoughts

AUGUST: FLOW

Element of Earth

Mookaite, by Krista Thornhill, 2014

For the Earth Table: apples, rocks, bowl of soil, a picture
or yourself

August: Flow

This month, Earth takes a step back and allows the sun its moment of glory. The garden is pretty much doing its own thing by now, only requiring watering, as we get to watch the plants max out their sun intake and grow to their fullest. It's exciting to watch the garden take over, to be able to sit back and enjoy the show and to trust that the Earth knows exactly what she's doing. She is in perfect control. It makes me think of children coming into their independence, not needing parents as much as they did. I catch myself thinking of the future and how this precious time with my children will soon change and I see the correlation with the Earth. Soon this growing season will be over, and it will be harvest time, the chaos of the season will begin to produce fruit, and then we must prepare to let go and ready ourselves for winter. In August, I often find myself dreaming of the future and wrestling with my inner demons that want me to fear change.

THE INTERNAL JOURNEY

Chaos

> *Chaos was the law of nature; order was the dream of man.*
>
> *The Education of Henry Adams* – Henry Adams

We tend to have this sense that chaos is bad. Order is something we try to impose upon chaos to make it fit our needs and requirements to feel effective, in control, and powerful. When we can accept that there is a force of nature that is beyond our control, we can find beauty in what appears chaotic, for we know that it is from this point of chaos that great change is born. It is in this natural chaos that we can embrace the wild nature within ourselves, enabling us to embrace change all the more easily. When we resist the chaos that change creates, we fight against a natural law.

Creating Flow

A whole new focus is rocking the world of psychology: the science of happiness.[49] New research purposes that happiness is not something achieved at the end of an event, but rather experienced during an event (i.e., happiness is a verb, not a noun). It leads us to consider that if happiness is not a destination, but rather an action, then how we are journeying becomes important. My favourite human psychologist, Mihaly Csikszentmihalyi, who I was introduced to in a Positive Psychology course, believes that happiness "becomes a circuitous path that begins with achieving control over the contents of our consciousness."[50] When we are in flow, we are experiencing a certain control over our situation; we know what we are doing and are confident in our ability to do it well. This sense of control is defined by Csikszentmihalyi as an *optimal*

---

49 positive psychology: psychological interventions that foster positive attitudes toward one's subjective experiences, individual traits, and life events; the goal is to minimize pathological thoughts that may arise in a hopeless mindset, and to, instead, develop a sense of optimism toward life

50 Mihaly Csikszentmihalyi, Flow: The Psychology of Optimal Experience (New York: Harper & Row: 1990), 3.

Experience, meaning that when we are completely in sync with what we are doing, we lose track of time, we feel in control of the situation, the act itself is reward enough and needs no prize at its completion.[51] An optimal experience is one in which we are fully engaged. These are the moments when we experience flow and when we truly are the happiest. Consider what things allow you to experience flow.

THE EXTERNAL JOURNEY

Lammas/Lughnassa: Festival of the Sun God

Celebrated August first is Lughnassa, the Gaelic festival marking the beginning of the harvest season. Also called Lammas, this day is all about celebrating the Divine Masculine! [52] What a magnificent job the sun has done all summer long, pumping out glorious heat, giving direction, making things grow! Now the sun will begin to draw back its power and reduce its impact upon the Earth; nights will grow a little longer, and a little cooler as the Earth takes over and bring things to fruition. To celebrate this solar gift, throw a Sun Party, full of competitive games, decorations, and feasts of roasted corn and hot baked cornbread in honour of the sun.

The bright one with a strong hand, Lugh was a great swordsman, harpist, and champion of the court for King Nuada[53] of the Tuatha Dé Danann.[54] He was also known as *the long arm* for his great skill with a

---

51 Ibid.

52 Lammas: traditionally a British celebration; the first of three harvest festivals in which bread are made from the first harvest of grain and given as an offering

53 King Nuada: King of the Tuatha Dé Danann for seven years before they went to Ireland

54 Tuatha Dé Danann: a race of supernaturally-gifted people in Irish mythology; thought to represent the main deities of pre-Christian Gaelic Ireland

sword. He is likened to the Greek God Apollo, the God of light and truth. A musician and athlete, Lugh was also associated with the sun. What a great myth to celebrate!

The Flying Up Moon

Also known as the Corn and Stugeon moon, this is my favourite moon of them all! The idea of flying totally lifts my spirits. The Cree people of Ontario, Canada called it the Flying Up Moon because it marked the time when young birds would take that last leap from their nest and fly onto new adventures. It feels like we are at the cusp of something great, may we have the courage to fly when its our turn to do so! This moons mantra is, I am ready to fly!"

KRISTA THORNHILL

A Place for Your Thoughts

A Place for Your Thoughts

SEPTEMBER: GRATITUDE

Element of Earth

Our First Harvest, by Krista Thornhill 2016

For the Earth Table: harvest vegetables, gourds, leaves, orange/red candles, pumpkins.

September: Gratitude

September calls us back to the work of receiving, as we engage in collecting the harvest of food and fruit. The element of Earth at its finest hour, as everything reaches its peak, the work changes, and we fall back into a routine that focuses our attention on preparations for winter.

Ah, the return of routine! With children's return to school comes every mother's deep sigh of relief! As one of the biggest transitions of the year, we went from the unscheduled chaos of summer to the routine and ordered structure of school.

Don't do anything extra or add more to your list until everyone is settled back into their routines. We can easily take on more than we should at this time: remember to keep it simple (it's acceptable to recycle backpacks and pencil cases and not to sign away all of your free time volunteering). Be careful not to hurry the process, as you have the whole month to adjust. Remember that the Fall Equinox, when light and dark become balanced once more, is soon upon us. Everything will fall into its natural order, so take your time and transition well.

THE INTERNAL JOURNEY

Discipline

In a world that caters to our whims and follies, discipline[55] is not a popular word or concept. When there is a quick fix out there for just about anything you want, applying ourselves diligently to achieve something is a concept I fear is being lost.

Discipline comes from training, working diligently to achieve, applying ourselves to that which we wish to obtain.[56] In my attempts to get healthy, I worked with a personal trainer three times a week for five months. She taught me how to exercise for my body structure and my weight goals. Truly I was in my prime; I loved how I felt in my body and the way my clothes fit the energy that I had. It was an amazing feeling.

Discipline comes out of a place of self-worth that says we are worth the effort; we are worthy of achieving our goals, we are worthy of obtaining that which we hope for, we are worthy of applying ourselves and working hard to get what we want. To be a disciple of life is to commit to it.

What goals do you have that require more discipline in your life?

Gratitude

Gratitude has the power to heal, change lives, and energize the soul.

I was blessed to hear Eckhart Tolle tell the following story about gratitude when he spoke at the Queen Elizabeth Theatre in Vancouver in

---

55 discipline: the suppression of base desires; usually understood to be synonymous with self-control, restraint, and control

56 to train: to teach a particular skill or type of behaviour through practice and instruction

April 2016: A student asked his Zen Master for advice before he left to go walking for a year to achieve enlightenment. The Zen Master said that to everyone he met, he must say, "Thank-you for everything. I have no complaints." [57]

A state of thankfulness is seeing the beauty in every challenge and knowing that everything happens for a reason, whether we are aware of the reason or not. Thankfulness opens you, expands you, and allows you to let go of your judgment and create the space for you to learn from everything that happens and from everyone you encounter.

A way to practice gratitude is to take all the negative things that have happened to us and look for ways for which to be grateful for them. Instead of blaming the past for all of the hardships you've experienced, focus on how they helped form who you are today. Even though my parents divorced when I was quite young and my dad moved away, I'm thankful he followed his dreams to go west because although it meant leaving us then, now we get to live on the West Coast of Canada and share our lives with him on a regular basis.

Boundaries

This month our time becomes more precious as we settle back into a routine. In nature, when things don't get harvested in time or processed in time, they rot. Time is of the essence when harvesting, making it all the more important for us to stay on task and enforce our own personal boundaries.[58] It's one thing to be available to others, but it's even more

---

57 Tolle, "The Power of Now" Speech.

58 personal boundaries: guidelines, rules or limits that a person creates to identify reasonable, safe, and permissible ways for other people to behave towards them and how they will respond when someone passes those limits

important to know when not to be available when it's time for your personal harvest. Reaping the rewards of a day well done means taking time for self on a daily basis.

Enforcing these boundaries helps us manage our time better and teaches all of us how to respect each other as individuals. The more you enforce them, the easier it gets –with yourself, family, friends, coworkers, bosses and even strangers. Know your limits. Know yourself. Know where to draw the line and when to make time for yourself!

This month as the harvest comes to its end and we ready ourselves for the descent into winter, create, enforce and maintain your boundaries. Know what is yours to protect and what is not. Fill your store rooms and stand guard.

THE EXTERNAL JOURNEY

Autumn Equinox: September 20-22

Balance is once again restored as days become equal with night. An equinox is an astronomical event in which the plane of the Earth's equator passes through the centre of the sun, which occurs twice a year, around the 20th of March and the 23rd of September. On an equinox, day and night are approximately equal. You can look forward to this time and celebrate it with a harvest meal, as by this time your family will have all successfully made the seasonal transition from summer into fall.

Engagement

Whether you have an inside fireplace, a fire pit outside, or neither, make a point of gathering an armful of wood or sticks when you are next out for a walk in nature. Gathering wood is a primal act that speaks deeply to our ancestral roots; there is something very cathartic and healing about gathering and carrying wood. This month, help a neighbour with their wood, cut a stack of kindling, or carve a walking stick to get your hands on some wood.

Visit a U-Pick to linger long amidst the fruit bushes, to sit and binge on your pickings and let the fruit juices run down your face and stain your fingers. With the remains of your harvest, make it your intention to turn them into something yummy. Make an apple pie or blueberry muffins from the fruit you harvest and share it with friends on Solstice. Doing something by hand and creating something to share is the very way you connect gratitude to this Season.

The Harvest Moon

Take a moment with this moon to ponder and reflect upon all your hard work. Let the moon draw forth from within you a deep sense of gratitude for the journey, the ups and the downs, the sacrifices and the blessings. What are you reaping this month? This moon's mantra is, "I am full. I want for nothing. I am complete. I am grateful."

A Place for Your Thoughts

KRISTA THORNHILL

A Place for Your Thoughts

A Place for Your Thoughts

OCTOBER: RELEASE

Element of Air

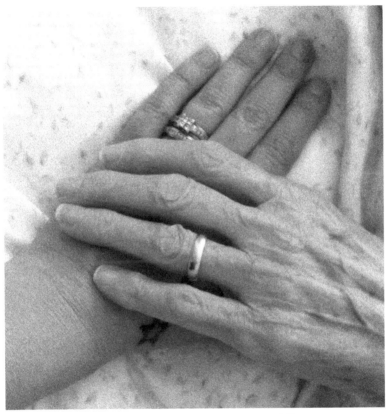

Where the Ocean Meets the Sky, by Krista Thornhill, 2013

For the Earth Table: ancestor memorabilia, bones, leaves and a vigil candle

October: Release

I was blessed to be with my darling grandmother as she surrendered all. I held her in my arms and watched the morning sun beam down on her face, her breathing slowed and steadied for the first time in days. She didn't gasp or fight, her heart just stopped beneath my hand on her chest, and with her last few breaths she opened her eyes and met mine. To birdsong and sunshine, her spirit completed its Earth Journey as I felt her last breath take flight. It was as if we witnessed an angel leave the room.

In October, Gaia prepares herself for her death. She releases the baggage as the trees drop their leaves, she gives away her treasures so that others can enjoy them, she lets the fruits of her labour be harvested and enjoyed by her children (though most of it will rot). She begins a slow descent of acceptance, readiness, and surrender as she prepares for the journey through to season's end. There is a somber and coolness to the air as October turns the wheel towards death.

Oh, how the winds of change blow down from the North and make us realize that summer is over and that all good things must come to their end.

THE INTERNAL JOURNEY

The Hunter

To hunt is to bring something living to its death so that it can be used for another purpose. It is the taking of life to preserve life, and it should never be done without this regard in mind. It should always be done consciously and in the best means possible, with much gratitude and humility of spirit. In Northern Alberta, hunting season brings a change in clothing attire, as camouflage is commonplace in browns, greens, and pinks. There is the smell of the hunt in the air; everyone is on a mission, and you cannot help but feel connected to the Earth as families head to open country to find food for the winter.

This hunting season is not specific to carnivores but calls each of us to examine and consider our lives, to seek out that which no longer serves us, something that needs to die. This is the greatest challenge of all, knowing when something is done, knowing when to quit and walk away. Just like taking the life of an animal should never come easy, this deep inspection of our lives calls us into conscious living. What will we offer up to death as she begins her descent upon the land?

The hunter energy is masculine; it is on task, focused, intent, it takes action to get what it wants. Before we set into winter, know what it is you want for yourself, for your family. Is it a holiday somewhere warm in March? Is it a new relationship or the end of one? Perhaps a course you need to complete in a series of studies? Is it new winter tires or a new coat? Whatever it is, hunt for it. Consider what needs to die and be let go of to receive the nourishment and fulfilment of the hunt. Tap into the masculine energy of the Hunter and claim what is yours!

The Goddess Artemis was the protector of Chastity, nurturer of life and yet also known as the Great Huntress.[59] The temple built in her honour became one of the Seven Wonders of the Ancient World. Artemis embodies all that is masculine, yet still holds the feminine. She is both the killer and the protector. It's not that we must choose one over the other, but that in balancing both, we can maximize the energies to achieve our goals. Use the energy of the season to give strength to your quest. What are you hunting? What needs to die so that something else might live? Tap into the sexy and deadly abundance of the hunter energy at this time.

The Death Eater

Soaring high above mountain peaks, larger than an eagle, the Condor, the mighty death eater, glides on the winds like a kite set free from tangles. It takes its time as it slowly circles, narrowing in on its prize as it descends, funneling gracefully, ever slowly down. Down through clouds, snow Alps, and past treetops, through light into darkness, it casts a growing shadow through the branches onto the forest floor below.

It knows the longer it takes, the riper the meat, and there's no fight that waits below, for its presence has already frightened off the smaller scavengers. With a grand swoop, the Condor lands, and claws into the meat and with its strong and fearsome beak, devours what has succumbed to death. With its belly full, it stretches out its magnificent wingspan and takes flight, up out of the lowest and darkest of valleys, carrying with it the spirit of that which was trapped in form. Up past the branches, up over mountaintops, and ever upwards to the sky, it carries spirit back from form. This is the job of the death eater.

---

59 Artemis: Greek Goddess of animals and hunting

At this time, connect with the energy of the great and mighty Condor. Use this imagery when facing big choices and having to let go of things that no longer serve you. Imagine if you will that what you leave behind to die gives way for new growth and new possibilities. Close your eyes and imagine the Condor descending for you, feel the rush of the Wind as its wings near you, feel the claw and the piercing that tears from you what is dead and feel the relief as this great and magnificent bird spreads its wings again and takes flight up over your head. Don't go into winter holding on to what has died; allow death to serve its purpose in your life.

THE EXTERNAL JOURNEY

Samhain[60] or All Hallows Eve: October 31st

> *The veil thins between the living and the dead, as the evening light casts early shadows upon the lawn. A misty fog blurs one's sight when treading between the stones. Ravens take flight and owls scream, in woods where fairies sing and on the plains coyotes howl. T'is the waking hours of the dead betwixt eerie dusk and creepy dawn.*

– Indira A. Ravynmoon, *unpublished writing*

The best pronunciation I have heard is *Sow-in*, the Gaelic celebration of harvest's end and the beginning of winter. Also celebrated as the Witches New Year's Eve, it is the night to visit with the Ancestors, to celebrate death, to don costumes, put out candy and keep evil spirits at

---

60 Samhain: a Gaelic festival marking the end of the harvest season and the beginning of winter or the "darker half" of the year

bay with jack-o'-lanterns. Westernized, this holiday became Halloween, also known as All Hallows Eve, with more focus on the evils of the spirit world as opposed to honouring the Ancestors. In some cultures, the jack-o'-lantern and decorations were a means for the deceased spirits to recognize their family homes and find their way back to their loved ones where they would find a place set for them at the table.

At this time of year, we bring out the pictures of our loved ones who have passed and set them about the house and on our Earth Table. In our home, it is a special time to tell stories and remember the ones we do not want ever to be forgotten, and we celebrate their presence still ever with us.

Celebrating Death

Admittedly death is a hard one to celebrate, but when we make a place for it in our lives annually by connecting with the Earth cycles and making room for it every year as the wheel turns, we make death much easier to embrace and even understand. No matter how painful, it becomes naturally incorporated into our lives and thus expected.

I believe it is the lack of invitation that disturbs us the most. Death's rude interruption takes us out of our living and demands, without apology, that we acknowledge and make room for it. If we are living ungrounded lives disconnected from Earth cycles, death will be the most unwelcome of all guests.

This October, set a place at the table for the unwelcome guest, align yourself with the Earth and grow to expect Death as she does. Not only does she expect it, but she also prepares for it. Don't be taken off guard and surprised when Death shows up at the door. Make a place for it in your life, celebrate it, anticipate it, and welcome it. Even through the tears and heartbreak, make peace with Death.

Hunter's Moon

In the light of this full moon, reach within yourself and ask for wisdom, what needs to be let go of? What needs to die in order for you to move on? The mantra for this last moon of our year's journey, "I release what no longer serves me. I am strong enough to let go."

KRISTA THORNHILL

A Place for Your Thoughts

A Place for Your Thoughts

KRISTA THORNHILL

A Place for Your Thoughts

A Place for Your Thoughts

In Summation

Such grace and ease have been brought into my life through living with the seasons. I have created compassion for myself and a much stronger sense of self-love by allowing myself to step in sync with her as I journey. I trust that there is indeed a time and a place for all the things I want to accomplish and experience and I no longer feel rushed, disconnected or ungrounded. Living with this Earth-based awareness has been the best medicine for me; it has provided healing from the symptoms of post-traumatic stress disorder, it has given me great inner peace, and it has provided me with a deep sense of assurance that I am on the right path. As a result, I no longer experience panic attacks or suffer from anxiety.

Earth-based living is not about belief or faith: it is about being able to know! I find great comfort in knowing that after winter comes spring. In that knowing, I can exercise faith, and I can have a belief that all things do have a divine timing, that everything happens for a reason, and that the wheel keeps turning. I know this to be true!

The Elemental Seasons: Understanding the Four Seasons

(As they relate to the Elements of the Earth)

The Season of Air: October, November, and December

> *"Air is the element of East, associated with thought and mind, with rising sun, with inspiration and enlightenment. Air is the breath of the Goddess, Her living inspiration."* The Earth Path, – Starhawk

As we bask in the harvest, enjoying the fruits of our labour, we reflect as the winds of change begin to blow and the leaves begin to fall; we remember and give thanks to our Ancestors for their words of wisdom spoken deep from within ourselves.

Air is the evidence of the unseen. We can see its movement as it passes through the trees, over the waters, and tosses about our hair. We can feel it upon our skin and be knocked down by its force.

The Season of Fire: January, February and March

We turn to the element of Fire and call forth its power of destruction, its courage, and its passion. We offer up what we have gleaned from our past; our stories and the ones of those that went before us, and we ask the Fires of change to burn away what needs to be purged from our lives. During these three winter months, we turn our focus inward and do the work of deep healing. Through journaling, quiet meditation, deep introspection, prayer, sacrifice, therapy, healing modalities and others, we tap into the energy of Fire to burn away and return to ashes what should no longer be. We connect with the energy of Fire to face our fears, to gain courage, and to awaken a deep sense of passion within for the life we have been given.

The Season of Water: April, May and June

We come out of the fires and slip into the cooling waters, where we wash away the ashes from our skin and the smell of smoke from our hair. These months are about purification, healing, and self-love as we let go of the past and move into the present, feeling good about the work we did in the dark months of winter. We will use this time to transition into summer empowered, rejuvenated, and healed. We have earned our right to celebrate the return of the sun.

The Season of Earth: July, August and September

Like every bath that eventually turns too cold to enjoy and causes fingertips to ripple like raisins, so too comes the time to step out of the waters and plant our feet on solid ground. We turn now to the element of Earth, where we seek grounding in our healing and live out all that we have learned. This time is all about how we choose to walk upon this Earth. Warm enough to walk barefoot, to swim in outdoor waters, and to sleep out under the stars, we are reminded of our relationship with Gaia as she invites us to engage and participate with her.

Introducing Krista

Island Priestess, Billie Woods Photography 2019

For seven years I visited with a psychiatrist, a woman I instantly wanted to treat like a grandmother, but despite her grey hair, she was ultimately NOT going to be her substitute.

She was a psychiatrist; removed, sharp-eyed and silent.

It was not her guidance, counsel or advice, nor the prescription I refused to take that healed me; it was her consistency, her objectivity, and her refusal to be emotionally manipulated by me that created the safe place for me to learn how to trust. She had very clear boundaries.

She was unwavering, neither kind nor mean, but temperate, just, stern and fair. It was her being true to herself and showing up relentlessly authentic, that allowed me to see myself with my own eyes and figure out my own stuff.

Committing to those fifty-minute sessions was the hardest part of the work. At first, I was excited to go, like somehow this was going to validate everything (meaning all my excuses), and I would finally have an ally to root me on in my chaotic and unrooted life. I quickly learned she was not going to be my cheer leader.

After seven years of my life story being written down in a note pad, there is only one piece of wisdom that she gave me that still sticks in my memory, the one that inspired this book. She looked me straight in the eye and said, "You know Krista, you really just needed to learn how to trust an older woman."

I thought that therapy was all about the recounting of injustices, stories of heart-break and misunderstandings, tales of abuse and neglect, and I could hardly under-stand how it was all supposed to help me. What she gave me instead was time. The time to run out of stories, time to lay all pretenses down, time to hear my own truth, time to learn how to trust myself and the time to realize I no longer needed her time.

Only in retrospect do I see what she meant by *trust* because I first needed to really be honest with myself and look at why I was unable to trust. I had to treat the immediate symptoms first. I had to begin by facing my current everyday issues, like lack of commitment, poor communication, tardiness, disorganization, drug addiction, and post-partum depression before I could ever get to deal with real side-effects of trauma, which would come up years later. These included disassociation, depression, addiction, obesity, anxiety, and ones I continue to work on daily.

I ponder on this memory, as it came racing to my mind as I started to write this book about meeting Mother Earth, and I hear the doctor's words ringing in my ears, "learn to trust an older woman." Admittedly, the whole *goddess path* thing was difficult for me to grasp in the beginning. Although all other pagan elements were easy to embrace, it's taken me a long time even to be comfortable with calling her *Mother Earth*.

Now, I am beginning to see the connection: my personal un-rootedness stemmed from what I now understand as the "mother wound."[61] This has actually very little to do with my own mother but more to do with the fact that the mothers of the world have been carrying deep generational wounds for centuries. And it's not just a female wound; men too have suffered greatly and thus perhaps experienced disconnect even more so.

> *For every human being, the very first wound of the heart*
> *was at the site of the mother, the feminine. And through*
> *the process of healing that wound, our hearts graduate*
> *from a compromised state of defensiveness and fear to a*

---

61 the mother wound: a matrilineal wound; a burden that manifests in mothers and is passed on from generation to generation

whole new level of love and power, which connects us to the divine heart of Life itself.

– Bethany Webster, *Why it's Crucial for Women to Heal the Mother Wound*

This concept of the feminine has taken me many years to process, embrace, and assimilate. Over the years it has been the key source of much inner healing, starting with learning about worth, being worth the effort and loving myself.

My life was in a state of chaos: when I began to awaken to the hard truths of my reality, I was spinning, I had no idea who I was or what I was doing. I felt caught in a vicious whirlwind. I suffered from a deep sense of disconnect; I was going from one mishap to the other, experiencing constant misfortune and stuck in a cloud of misery feeling completely sorry for myself, un-empowered and worthless.

As I became aware of this disconnection, I began to notice all the pagan gatherings that were happening in my community, the ones I'd only heard about after they'd been celebrated, all those solstices and equinox gatherings I would miss and full moon circles after the fact. I recognized within me this feeling like I was trying to catch up, feeling left behind and out of sync with my life. I was completely unrooted, discombobulated, and at the end of a marriage. I knew I desperately needed some soul intervention.

To save my sanity, I started taking long walks again by myself. Many times I was in full stint to get away from the house. I took long moments to sit in the sunshine, to stop and listen. I gardened all day until it was dark and even then I would persist. I built my own fires and sat by them alone, my back to the dark forest, and I lingered long in the moonlight and took walks when the moon was new. It was in those moments full of natural noise that helped quiet my racing mind, and it was taking this space that brought me home, home to myself. Thankfully all I needed to do was go outside and look up at the moon.

If I were going to create change in my life, real change that would give me the grounding and the rootedness that I was desperately craving, I would have to start there in that very moment, in the quiet of the outdoors, a divorced mother of two, staring at the moon. I did not know who I was or how I had gotten myself into such a mess. The one thing that certainly was true, the one absolute I had left, was that first and foremost, I was a woman, and gazing into the face of a filling moon, I realized my journey would start with healing the feminine. For there is no older woman than the Earth herself.

Earth and I have been on a journey together and have become good friends. The more I understand her, the more I understand myself, and the more I understand myself, the more I need her.

A Parting Wish

Just like the lilies of the field and the birds of the air have no worries, we too can be assured and confident that all of our needs will be met. When you can anticipate, participate, and celebrate the changing of the seasons, all parts of your life line up and begin to make sense.

May you feel the wind upon your face, know the ground beneath your feet, soak in the heat of a good fire and be baptized by the cleansing powers of water. May you know daily the presence of peace and feel grounded on your journey. May you reach ever taller for better sight of the stars and know that you are here for a purpose; an earth based spirit having a human experience and this too, one day, shall pass.

Blessings on Your Journey,

Krista

Bibliography

Carroll, Lewis. "Alice in Wonderland" in *Lewis Carroll: The Complete Works*.

London: CRW Publishing Limited, 2005.

Csikszentmihalyi, Mihaly. *Flow: The Psychology of Optimal Experience*. New York: Harper and Row: 1990.

Higginbotham, Joyce, and River Higginbotham. *Christo Paganism: An Inclusive Path*. Minnesota: Llewellyn Publications, 2009.

Peck, Scott M. *The Road Less Travelled*. New York: Simon and Schuster, 1987.

"Positive Psychology and the Science of Happiness." Pursuit of Happiness. December 15, 2016. Accessed May 23, 2017. http://www.pursuit-of-happiness.org/science-of-happiness/.

Practical Magic. Directed by Griffin Dunne. Los Angeles, CA: Village Roadshow Pictures, 1998.

Service, Robert W. "The Cremation of Sam McGee." Poetry Foundation. Accessed May 15, 2017. https://www.poetry-foundation.org/poems-and-poets/poems/detail/45081.

Shakespeare, William. "A Midsummer Night's Dream," in *William Shakespeare: The Complete Works*. New York: Barnes and Nobel, Inc., 1994.

Starhawk, Baker, Diane, and Anne Hill. *Circle Round: Raising Children in the Goddess Tradition*. New York: Bantam Books, 1998.

Starhawk, Baker, Diane, and Anne Hill. "The Rebirth of the Sun," in *Circle Round: Raising Children in the Goddess Tradition*. New York: Bantam Books, 1998.

Starhawk. *The Earth Path: Grounding Your Spirit in the Rhythms of Nature*. New York: Harper San Francisco, 2004.

Tanzi, Rudolph E., and Deepak Chopra. *The Super Brain*. New York: Three Rivers Press, 2012.

Thornhill, Krista. "*Beach Treasure*" Instagram Post. March 11, 2017. https://www.instagram.com/p/BRhKMNVhMd2/?taken-by=krista_thornhill_stel

Thornhill, Krista. "*Christmas Stories*." Instagram Post. July 14, 2016. https://www.instagram.com/p/-5bh_Au3IF/?taken-by=krista_thornhill_stel

Thornhill, Krista. "*Colleen*." 1992. Montego Bay, Jamaica. Personal Collection

Thornhill, Krista. "*God was a Woman. Bev Yeoman's Chair*." Instagram Post. November 4, 2013. https://www.instagram.com/p/gUe1-Ou3Nh/?taken- by=krista_thornhill_stel

Thornhill, Krista. "*Hide and Seek Frog.*" Instagram Post. August 19, 2016. Salt Spring Is. BC https://www.instagram.com/p/BJS9BpcgSwm/?taken- by=krista_thornhill_stel

Thornhill, Krista. "*Mookaite.*" Instagram post. August 21, 2015. Galiano Is. BC https://www.instagram.com/p/6qbqVGO3JR/?taken-by=krista_thornhill_stel

Thornhill, Krista. "*Our First Harvest.*" Instagram Post. September 13, 2016. Salt Spring Is. BC https://www.instagram.com/p/BKUxdFhghZv/?taken-by=krista_thornhill_stel

Thornhill, Krista. "*Pink Roses from My Daughter.*" Instagram Post. August 28, 2016. https://www.instagram.com/p/BJraKoggPHE/?taken-by=krista_thornhill_stel

Thornhill, Krista. "*Poppy and his wife Eudora walking through Ruckle Park*" Salt Spring Is. BC Instagram Post. November 17, 2016. https://www.instagram.com/p/BM8P5N4gv1W/?taken- by=krista_thornhill_stel

Thornhill, Krista. "*Sage & Lavender.*" Salt Spring Is. BC Instagram Post. July 6, 2016. https://www.instagram.com/p/BHids7vA4qw/?taken-by=krista_thornhill_stel

Thornhill, Krista. "*Shells & Broken Glass.*" Instagram Post. March 11, 2017.

https://www.instagram.com/p/BRhKMNVhMd2/?taken-by=krista_thornhill_stel

Thornhill, Krista. "*Smudging the Garden*" Instagram Post. February 19, 2017. Salt Spring Is. BC https://www.instagram.com/p/BQt7PKaBRKZ/?taken-by=krista_thornhill_stel

Thornhill, Krista. "*The Green Family's Earth Table.*" 2015. Salt Spring Is. BC Personal Collection.

Thornhill, Krista. "*Unconditional.*" Instagram Post. October 20, 2016. Salt Spring Is. BC https://www.instagram.com/p/BLz1wgLgKr_/?taken-by=krista_thornhill_stel

Thornhill, Krista. *Where the Ocean Meets the Sky.*" May 12, 2013. Personal Ccollection, St. John's, Newfoundland.

Tolle, Eckhart. "The Power of Now." Speech, Vancouver, BC, April 16th, 2016.

Webster, Bethany. "Why it's Crucial for Women to Heal the Mother Wound." The Womb of Light- The Work of Bethany Webster. Accessed May 17, 2017. http://www.womboflight.com/why-its-crucial-for-women-to-heal-the-mother-wound/.

Woods, Billie. "*Island Priestess*" Billie Woods Photography, Salt Spring Island BC Aprils 2019 http://www.billiewoods.com

Index

If you have enjoyed Earth Journey and would like to go deeper, you are invited to avail of Krista's other offerings.

Connect deeper with your own personal power by learning the ways of the earth, aligning with the seasons and mastering you own intuitive ability to guide and ground yourself on this magical earth journey.

INTO THE RIVER

Element of Water

Where does one begin to heal the past? How do we reconcile our heritage with our present world realities and how do we purge the religious baggage and expand beyond what we were taught?

Designed to expand beyond your religious upbringing and help you step out of the past and on to your own unique spiritual path, Into the River provides a safe opportunity for you to reclaim your spiritual heritage, make peace with your past while acknowledging your present realities, and gain confidence in your own ability to discern for yourself what is true, relevant and important to you.

This course explores different possibilities, considers new ways to understand Christian history and invites you to consider what it means to really experience heaven on earth.

It is our personal responsibility to ask questions, to broaden our perspectives and to seek god in the impossible.

This six week course provides; a reading list, six chapter downloads, six videos delivering the material, weekly check ins and an invite to join a private face book group for sharing and community building with others who have come "Into the River."

Available only May to July.

GAIA'S NIGHT JOURNEY

Element of Air and Fire

You are invited to join Krista for her Winter Journey starting every November, a deep intensive and inclusive path sharing as we travel through the dark half of the year, fully engaged with the power of the elements, moving forward together.

Deepen your relationship with yourself, your ancestors and with Gaia over the six months of winter by, diving deeper into the elements of air and fire, learning how to avail of them, working with mythology and implementing a practice of self-love and patience. We go into the Night together; holding space for each other, serving as each other's flashlights, learning as we go, sharing the dark road together stepping in sync with Gaia.

This intimate six month journey with Krista comes with downloadable weekly workbooks, weekly zoom group meetings, private face book group for sharing and community building and full access to Krista throughout the journey for support and mentorship.

***

To subscribe to Krista's monthly newsletter, The Spoke and to inquire about journeying with her personally, please visit her website www.kristathornhill.com and/or send an email to

krista@earthbasedspirit.com. She would love to hear from you!
Join her community of likeminded spirits on face book for daily nuggets on creating an earth based awareness, look for Earth Based Spirits and come join us!

"If you want to go fast, go alone. If you want to go far, go together."

~African proverb

CPSIA information can be obtained
at www.ICGtesting.com
Printed in the USA
BVHW060938080323
659876BV00003B/30

9 781525 560941